W9-BTS-408

DATE			

WITHDRAWN

Pebble® Plus

Health and Your Body

MyPlate and You

by Gillia M. Olson

CAPSTONE PRESS
a capstone imprint

Pebble Plus is published by Capstone Press,
1710 Roe Crest Drive, North Mankato, Minnesota 56003.
www.capstonepub.com

Books published by Capstone Press are manufactured with paper
containing at least 10 percent post-consumer waste.

Library of Congress Cataloging-in-Publication Data
Olson, Gillia M.
  MyPlate and you / by Gillia M. Olson.
    p. cm. — (Pebble plus. Health and your body)
  Summary: "Color photos and simple text describe the MyPlate plan for healthy eating"— Provided by publisher.
  Includes bibliographical references and index.
  ISBN 978-1-4296-6809-5 (library binding) — ISBN 978-1-4296-7129-3 (paperback)
  1. Nutrition—Juvenile literature. 2. Food—Juvenile literature. 3. Health—Juvenile literature. I. Title. II. Series.
  RA784.O47 2012
  613.2—dc22   2011005139

Editorial Credits

Kyle Grenz, designer; Marcie Spence, media researcher; Sarah Schuette, photo stylist; Marcy Morin, studio scheduler;
    Laura Manthe, production specialist

Photo Credits

Capstone Studio: Karon Dubke, 1, 5, 7, 9, 11, 13, 15, 17, 19, 20, 21
Shutterstock: Arvind Balaraman, cover
USDA/MyPlate.com, cover, 5 (MyPlate icon)

Note to Parents and Teachers

The Health and Your Body series supports national standards related to health and physical
education. This book describes and illustrates how to use MyPlate. The images support early
readers in understanding the text. The repetition of words and phrases helps early readers learn
new words. This book also introduces early readers to subject-specific vocabulary words, which are
defined in the Glossary section. Early readers may need assistance to read some words and to use
the Table of Contents, Glossary, Read More, Internet Sites, and Index sections of the book.

Printed in the United States of America in North Mankato, Minnesota.
032012
006645R

Table of Contents

Author's Note: Serving sizes are based on
recommendations for children ages 4 to 8.

Healthy Eating

MyPlate teaches people about healthy eating. This guide shows how much to eat from each food group every day.

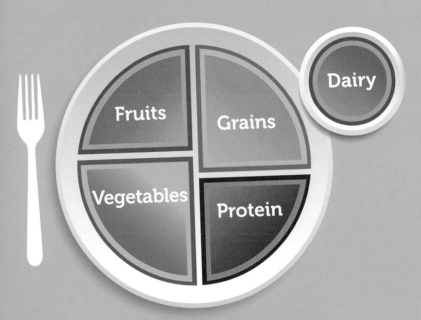

ChooseMyPlate.gov

Grain Group

Grains are seeds such as wheat, rice, and oats. Kids should eat 4 to 5 ounces from this group each day. Half should be whole grains.

Vegetable Group

Eat vegetables for lots
of vitamins and minerals.
Kids need 1 ½ cups a day.
During a week, eat different
vegetables for different vitamins.

Fruit Group

Fruit grows on vines, bushes, and trees. Fruit also contains lots of vitamins and minerals. Kids need 1 to 1 ½ cups of fruit every day.

Dairy Group

The dairy group includes

milk, cheese, and yogurt.

Milk has calcium and protein

for strong bones and muscles.

Kids need 2 cups each day.

Protein Group

The protein group includes
meat, beans, nuts, eggs, and
other foods full of protein.
Eat 3 to 4 ounces each day
from this group to grow strong.

Fats and Sugars

Most people eat more fat
and sugar than they need.
Choose low-fat foods
as much as possible.
Avoid foods with added sugar.

Being Active

Being active is part of being healthy. Kids should be active at least 60 minutes a day. Exercise plus healthy foods will keep you healthy.

Fun Facts

- Popcorn is considered a grain.
  It's made from kernels, or seeds,
  of corn. But fresh corn is considered
  a vegetable.

- You can eat a burger without eating
  meat. Veggie burgers are made from
  vegetables or beans.

- Most sodas have equal to 3 or 4 tablespoons of sugar in them.

- The average person drinks about 23 gallons of milk each year. A person eats about 30 pounds of cheese each year too.

- Dry beans include kidney beans, soybeans, and lima beans. They are part of both the vegetable group and the protein group. That's because they have much more protein than most other vegetables.

Glossary

active—busy or moving around

calcium—a mineral that the body uses to build teeth and bones

mineral—a solid material found in nature that is not made by animals or plants, but can be taken in and used by animals or plants to stay healthy

muscle—a part of the body that makes movement; muscles are attached to bones

protein—a substance found in plant and animal cells

vitamin—a substance found in food or made in the body that is needed to stay healthy

whole grain—a food using all parts of a grain seed; other grain foods may use only part of the seed

Read More

Dickmann, Nancy. *Fruits.* Healthy Eating. Chicago: Heinemann Library, 2011.

Kalman, Bobbie. *I Eat a Rainbow.* My World. New York: Crabtree Pub. Co., 2010.

Lee, Sally. *Healthy Snacks, Healthy You!* MyPlate and Healthy Eating. Mankato, Minn.: Capstone Press, 2012.

Internet Sites

FactHound offers a safe, fun way to find Internet sites related to this book. All of the sites on FactHound have been researched by our staff.

Here's all you do:

Visit *www.facthound.com*

Type in this code: 9781429668095

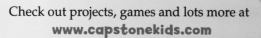

Super-cool stuff! Check out projects, games and lots more at **www.capstonekids.com**

Index

Word Count: 193 (main text)

Grade: 1

Early-Intervention Level: 17